HACKNEY LIBRARY SERVICES

Please return this book to any library in Hackney, on or
before the last date stamped. Fines may be charged if it is late.
Avoid fines by renewing the book (subject to it NOT being reserved).

Call the renewals line on 020 8356 2539

People who are over 60, under 18 or registered disabled
are not charged fines.

PJ42014

The Colourful World of

Clarice Cliff

Howard and Pat Watson

The Colourful World of Clarice Cliff

Acknowledgements

Grateful thanks to Stella Beddoe, of the Royal Pavilion, Art Gallery and Museums, Brighton, Jonathan Campbell, Jane Cook and Gary Withey, Mike Harvey, Muir Hewitt, Irene and Gordon Hopwood, Des Jones, Kathy Niblett of the City Museum and Art Gallery, Stoke-on-Trent, and the staff of Stoke-on-Trent City Library, Rosemary and David Temperley, Annie and Ian Tickler, Diana York and other anonymous friends. Also, for the use of photographs, Philip Bartlam of 'Antique Dealer and Collectors Guide', John Steel of the Antique Collectors Club Ltd. and Ward Lock Ltd., as well as to the very helpful staff of Christie's, Michael Newman of Plymouth, Phillips, Sotheby's Chester and Sotheby's Sussex, and to all other friends, especially Ruth Enock, Jean May and Winifred Wigner, who gave us time to write.

Photography

Unless otherwise indicated, all photography is by Simon Photography, Warwick.

Published by Kevin Francis Publishing

85 Landcroft Rd, LONDON SE22 9JS, ENGLAND
&
32246 Oakview, Warren, Michigan 48092, USA

Produced & Designed by **Francis Salmon**
Compiled by **James Scannell**
Editorial **Clare Ling**
© Howard and Pat Watson and Kevin Francis Publishing 1992

Printed by Greenwich Press London

Important Notice

All the information in this book has been compiled from reliable sources and every effort has been made to eliminate errors and questionable data. Nevertheless the possibility of error always exists. The publisher and authors will not be held responsible for losses which may occur in the purchase, sale or other transaction of items because of information contained herein. Readers who feel they have discovered errors or who would like to offer further information are invited to write to the authors via the publisher's address.

Contents

Clarice Cliff – The Sunshine Girl   5

Collecting Clarice Cliff   11

Surface Techniques   12

Backstamps   14

Examples of Backstamps   17

Gallery

I	Decorative Finishes	18
II	Facemasks and Figurines	38
III	Novelty Items	46
IV	Commissioned work	53
V	Tableware Shapes	58
VI	Rare Shapes and Patterns	65
VII	Shape Guide	97

General Price Guide   102

Clarice Cliff Chronology   104

Appendix - Auction Trends   106

Bibliography   106

Index to Patterns   107

KEY:
Original Patterns and Range Names - Bold
Modern Pattern Names - Lower Case
Shape Names - *Italics*

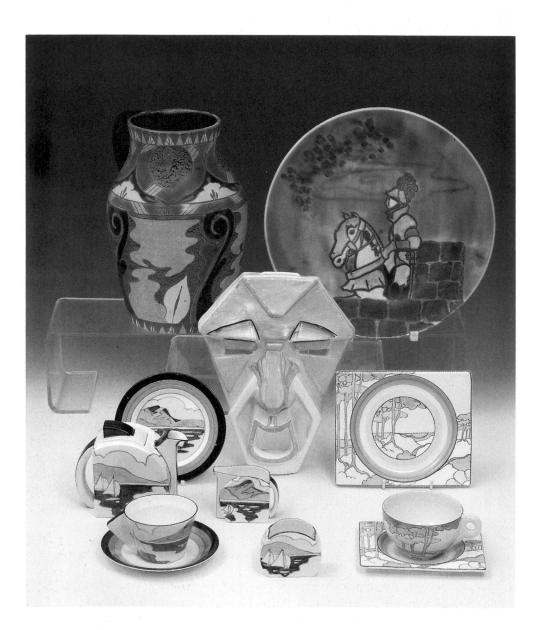

Courtesy of Sotheby's Sussex

Clarice Cliff,
The Sunshine Girl

They called her *the Sunshine Girl*, and the colourful hand-painted pottery she designed was hailed as *Happy China*. Today Clarice Cliff needs no introduction to collectors of Art Deco ceramics, and media attention has made her name once more a household word. One of the outstanding women designers of her era, she was internationally famous during her own lifetime and lived to see her pottery beginning to be eagerly collected in the early Seventies. Her prolific range of patterns and shapes and her fairy-tale life story have made her into a Potteries legend, and her facsimile signature now guarantees a good price - sometimes a sensationally high price - when it turns up at a London auction or on the Antiques Roadshow.

Though she was born in the final year of the last century there was nothing remotely Victorian about Clarice Cliff. Her ideas were well in advance of her own day, and though often imitated since have never been surpassed. She grew up, along with two brothers and five sisters, in a typical Potteries working-class family in Tunstall, Stoke-on-Trent. In later years she remembered as the high-spot of her schooldays the weekly half- hour drawing lessons and being "entrusted to make large papier mâché maps built up on nails of varying heights, and coloured, for use in geography lessons". At thirteen, like most children in the area, she left school to go to work, taking up an apprenticeship at Lingard, Webster and Company, to be taught free-hand painting on pottery. From there, she went to another factory, Hollingshead and Kirkham, to learn lithography, a form of transfer decoration, finally moving in 1916 to Wilkinson's Royal Staffordshire Pottery, where she was to remain for the rest of her career. In the evenings she went to classes at the Tunstall School of Art and on Sundays she taught at the local Sunday School. A vivacious brunette, she had a flair for stylish dressing, making many of her own clothes herself, and for interior decoration. Orange, yellow, gold and black were the colours she chose for her bedroom, which must have made it unique in the backstreets of Tunstall.

At Wilkinsons the apprentices were given training in modelling, gilding, firing and pottery design, along with the keeping of shape and pattern books. The decorating manager, Jack Walker, kept an eye on their developing skills and guided them into the department best suited to their talents. After seeing a free-hand picture of a butterfly painted in a spare moment by Clarice Cliff, and following a consultation with Colley Shorter, the firm's managing director, he put her to work alongside two of his chief designers, Fred Ridgeway and

John Butler. Her task was "very fine filigree gilding with a pen, tracing spiders' webs, butterflies etc. to hide small imperfections on expensive ware". Now in her mid-twenties, this gave her a certain amount of status, as well as increased wages, which meant she could afford to take the step, unusual for those days, of moving into a flat of her own. In no time she had transformed it to suit her advanced ideas - a pink and blue bedroom, a bathroom in yellow and black.

Even more important was the decision on the part of the management to send her for a short course in sculpture at the Royal College of Art in London. There she worked hard, creating a good impression on the authorities. Her course tutor, Professor Ledward, reported that "she has natural ability as a modeller ... and would derive very great benefit from a longer period of continuous study". The Registrar also considered that there was "no doubt that she has native ability" and wrote to assure Colley Shorter that "we should be pleased to admit her again". Eager to put her new ideas into practice, Clarice returned to the Potteries, where she now had a studio awaiting her at Newport Pottery, adjoining Wilkinson's main factory. Since its takeover by Wilkinsons in 1920, shelves piled high with dated stocks of whiteware had gathered dust in Newport Pottery, but now its time had come. "This huge stock," Clarice Cliff wrote years later,"had always interested me, and presented a challenge!". In rising to that challenge she transformed not only her own career but the fortunes of her employers, then at a low ebb, and in so doing earned for herself a place in the history of British pottery.

The Birth of Bizarre

Faced by the dusty whiteware, Clarice visualised it transformed by the application of bright colours in bold geometric designs. Beginning with diamonds, triangles and banding in a variety of combinations, the patterns she devised were within the limited capabilities of the young apprentices who could be spared to take part in the experiment. Considerable care was taken to preserve secrecy, and not until over seven hundred pieces had been decorated was the range launched, in the Autumn of 1928, under the name of **Bizarre Ware**, chosen by Clarice herself. Her own name was added to the backstamp, an accolade which put her on equal terms with the select band of acknowledged ceramic artists like Charlotte Rhead, Susie Cooper and Mollie Hancock. Not everyone at the factory was so confident, however - the firm's salesmen, used to taking traditional patterns round to their customers, regarded the new range with doubt and derision. To their astonishment they found that on a trial run it was welcomed as an attractive novelty, and sold quickly. More paintresses were added to the Bizarre team and the patterns and colours were standardised to speed up production. Variations on the regular geometric designs led to the use of sweeping curves and blocks of strong colour in abstract shapes to satisfy the demand for "colour and plenty of it ... I cannot put too much of it into my designs to please women", as Clarice herself said at the time. Continual change, too, she knew, was the order of the day. All the pottery manufacturers in the area - and there were four hundred factories competing for orders - constantly brought out new ranges to catch the customer's eye, ranges they advertised in the trade journal, the *Pottery Gazette and Glass Trades Review* and which they put on display at the annual London trade fairs and in the leading department stores. Before long, Clarice and her Bizarre Girls were travelling the country to give in-store demonstrations of their methods, so that the public and the press could admire the skill which went into the production of this exciting new range.

For Clarice Cliff, of course, the success of Bizarre Ware meant much more than commercial viability, important though that was. It is difficult today, with very different social attitudes, to imagine how much was at stake personally for her. Its creation had involved her in many weeks of close co-operation with Colley Shorter, a much older married man with an invalid wife, and inevitably their growing intimacy had become the subject of speculation and gossip on the part of workers and the management team alike. Had Colley Shorter formed an association with a woman considered to be his social equal and well away from the factory setting, probably little notice would have been taken of the situation, under the circumstances. As it was, Clarice had laid herself open to barely-concealed disapproval on all sides, and if she failed the future looked bleak. There would be many jealous observers only too glad to see her taken down a peg or two. Only success, overwhelming success, could ensure her survival, and fortunately her gamble paid off. Her relief must have been enormous - she had succeeded beyond her wildest dreams. At last a secure future lay ahead, ending eventually, after his wife's death, in marriage to the man who had trusted in her talent and launched her on her brilliant career. No wonder she worked long and hard to ensure that her success continued: she was spurred on by the knowledge that things might easily have been very different indeed.

Crocus and After

Floral patterns followed the early geometric and abstract designs, starting with the **Crocus** range, which was so popular that **Lupin**, next to it in the pattern book, was never put into full production and is now extremely rare. In its various colourways, on both conventional existing shapes and on the striking modern shapes Clarice designed herself, **Crocus** had a lively immediate appeal which made it a continuous best-seller throughout the Thirties. More floral patterns - **Gayday, Lily, Gardenia** and **Cowslip** - were added, and as the skills of her paintresses increased Clarice introduced stylised landscapes, many of them featuring quaint cottages nestled among colourful trees and bushes. By now all the main stores and china shops across the country stocked her ware, and such was the demand that a new name, **Fantasque**, was coined for part of Newport's output.

"**Bizarre** was usually sold to one customer in a town, so **Fantasque** was supposed to be a little different and sold to another shop", she wrote. Experiments in decorative techniques and surface textures led to new variations such as **Latona** and **Inspiration** (1929), **Scraphito**, **Applique** and **Delecia** (1930), **Cafe au Lait**, **Nuage** and **Damask Rose** (1931) and **Patina** (1932). As fashions changed, the hard-edged hand-painting technique was supplemented by the softer 'etching' a blending of brush-strokes used for patterns like **Rhodanthe**, **Viscaria**, **Aurea** and **Tralee** (1934-5) and the moulded ranges, **My Garden** and **Celtic Harvest**, came into their own.

Besides the tableware, vases and plaques that were the bread-and-butter lines of the factory, facemasks, figurines and novelty items appeared in a continuous stream, evidence that Clarice Cliff had never lost her interest in and enjoyment of modelling in clay. From time to time, too, this was combined with experiments with glazes, so that some pieces were issued in a commercial combination of colours, like cream and gilt, but also in a restrained celadon grey-green. The **Goldstone** range, too, though usually found with rather crude decoration, can sometimes be seen with simple lining which looks stunningly modern and sophisticated.

Although Wilkinsons and Newport Pottery were both in the happy position of full order-books, the state of the industry overall was giving cause for concern. In 1932 an experiment was initiated which was designed to involve leading artists of the day in creating patterns for use on pottery and china. The collaboration between Laura Knight and Clarice Cliff was particularly fruitful and these are the pieces which today fetch very high prices. At the time, however, the experiment was not a success, partly because, however famous, the artists lacked confidence in designing for an unknown medium and so tended to be timid, and partly because the public did not respond with much enthusiasm, perhaps feeling that they were having highbrow art foisted upon them in disguise. Only a very few of the items in this range can match up to the originality and exuberance of Clarice Cliff's own designs, and no doubt she found it frustrating to have to spend so much time on an exercise she may well have realised from the start was doomed to failure.

The Later Years

Though her earliest ranges were gradually phased out, **Fantasque** in 1934 and **Bizarre** in 1937, Clarice's own success continued right up until the outbreak of war at the end of 1939. Colley Shorter's marketing expertise meant that she was constantly in the public eye and that her many celebrity customers from the world of stage, screen and radio were shown in the press at the factory or at London trade shows collecting goods they had ordered. The firm's scrap-book, now in the Wilkinson Archives at Stoke-on-Trent City Library, Hanley, is full of photographs and press cuttings of these occasions, which must have made a welcome break in the daily routine. Popular women's magazines like 'Woman's Journal' commissioned exclusive sets of dinner and tea-ware for their readers, and carried embroidery transfers and crochet patterns for table-mats or afternoon tea-cloths to complement Clarice Cliff pottery.

For their time, it seems likely that Wilkinsons were on the whole good employers. Though like most factories of the day the workshops were dark and dismal, the Bizarre Girls were allowed a radio and sang while they worked, a concession which sent production up by twenty-five per cent. Works outings were arranged to local beauty spots, and the firm took part in the 'Crazy Day' carnival parades in aid of charity. Trips to give demonstrations in London and elsewhere varied the routine for some of the girls, and thanks to the constant demand for their skills they all had job security, which meant a lot in those days. The paintresses had a certain status as members of the Bizarre team, and if they later remembered Clarice as a stickler for time-keeping and strict in her insistence on quality control, this made good business sense and ultimately was for their benefit. Anyone who remembers the factory floors of the Thirties knows that long hours, low wages and grim working conditions were the norm, not only in the Potteries.

Certainly there is no denying that Clarice worked as hard as anyone. With over two thousand patterns to her credit, as well as around five hundred new shapes, she had a formidable volume of work behind her when war came and the main factory was turned over to the production of undecorated hotel-ware, Newport becoming a government store. Her vivid colours and unexpected shapes had brightened the whole decade, had kept her employers on an even keel and ensured that the shadow of the dole queue never threatened her fellow-workers.

Drawing her inspiration, like all designers, from everything that came her way (the Staffordshire countryside, gardening books and art magazines to name but a few), she had kept up a constant creative output week in, week out. Now came the opportunity to settle down at last. With the death of Colley Shorter's wife, marriage soon followed and she became the mistress of a superb Art Nouveau house set in beautiful grounds. Though she continued to work on the administrative side of the factory for a time after the war, she sold the business to Midwinters shortly after being widowed in 1963 and devoted herself to her home and garden. In 1972, the year of her death, an exhibition of her work at Brighton Museum marked the beginning of the Clarice Cliff revival, and she provided notes for the catalogue and several pieces for display. More than forty years had passed since she launched her *Happy China* on an unsuspecting world. No doubt she smiled to think that what had then been a commercial gamble and a personal triumph was now part of pottery history, and that Clarice Cliff, the Sunshine Girl, had become the doyenne of Art Deco.

Pat Watson

Collecting Clarice Cliff

One of the most intriguing aspects of collecting Clarice Cliff is the knowledge that it was originally regarded as cheap, cheerful pottery for practical use in the home. Bought in vast quantities in the Thirties, few realised how popular the quirky colours and bold designs would become - not only as 'happy' household items, but artistic treasures admired by thousands of collectors worldwide.

At the same time, it was at variance with the conventional tableware of the day, and putting it on the market at all was a gamble. Sheer chance, backed up by a clever advertising strategy, meant that what began as an experiment quickly turned into a phenomenon. The name **Bizarre** says it all.

With the benefit of hindsight, it is easy to trace all kinds of influences which may have played a part in providing inspiration for particular shapes and patterns. Like all commercial designers, Clarice Cliff studied current trends and fashions, altering them to suit her purpose and taking into account the limitations of her material and the skills of her work-force. Her designs increased in complexity as production gathered momentum - from geometric to abstract, from abstract to floral, from floral to landscape - always with colour lavishly used to brighten up the drab interiors of her day.

The sensational success of **Bizarre Ware**, particularly in a period of economic hardship, is proof enough that Clarice Cliff shrewdly assessed the climate of the times and was fulfilling a need for colourful and original pottery which stood out from the tableware on offer from other manufacturers in the industry. Not afraid to take risks, she offered bored housewives something new, and in so doing created patterns and shapes which were to hold their appeal for all time.

For collectors today, particularly the design conscious, her work has many attractions. Unlike buyers in the Thirties, we now have the whole range at once to choose from, an endless variety of individual items, all instantly recognisable and each with its own special characteristics. Limited only by considerations of space and price-range, we can select the pieces we prefer from more than 2000 patterns and 500 shapes, and seldom these days does the functional purpose enter into a purchase. When did you last put lupins in your **Lotus** jug, or teabags into your *Stamford* teapot?

An added pleasure is the search. Not for us the routine shopping trip into the Thirties High Street to a china shop with shelves crammed with brand new Clarice Cliff pottery. Instead we have the excitement of the early morning arrival at the antiques fair, the long hours spent at the auction house, the leisurely browsing while on holiday, any of which may yield an unforeseen treasure, or equally, prove fruitless. No jumble-sale can be passed by, no junk shop, however unpromising, can be left unexplored, for, as every collector is aware, you never know ...

We all have our own great 'finds', that elusive piece with only the faintest hairline tucked away on the top shelf of the local charity shop, or the incredible discovery at the school fête, with only a few slight chips. Collectors are the eternal optimists, like avid gardeners who believe in the pictures on the front of seed-packets. And who can blame them? For after all, whatever the weather may be elsewhere, in the world of Clarice Cliff, the sun is always shining.

Surface Techniques

Hand-painted pottery, especially on-glaze hand-painting, has a spontaneity impossible to obtain by mechanical means.

Part of the charm of Clarice Cliff pottery lies in the minute variations which resulted from the pattern being copied by different paintresses at different times. The original design was copied from the pattern book, but as speed was the inevitable priority due to piecework rates, the paintresses sometimes worked from memory. This lead to slight changes in outline, but did not affect colours as they were standardised.

The hand-painting was carried out on ware previously glazed with 'Honeyglaze', a warm cream glaze specially mixed for Bizarre Ware. After decoration, the ware was fired for 12 hours to harden the enamel paint used.

Patterns like **Crocus** were painted in colour, free-hand, but more elaborate patterns were first outlined in Indian ink, which evaporated during firing. Varieties of **Crocus** included **Original Crocus** (sometimes called **Autumn Crocus**), in purple, blue and orange, **Spring Crocus** in pastel shades, **Sungleam** in orange and yellow, **Blue Crocus** and **Purple Crocus** in single colours and **Peter Pan Crocus**, which was the original design with a black silhouette of a tree added. Later variations included placing the croci in a bunch at the side of the ware, and even coming downwards from the rims of cups and jugs.

Other glazes besides 'Honeyglaze' were used to create special effects for new ranges. **Latona** was a milky glaze with an egg-shell finish which, combined with a number of specifically designed floral and geometric patterns that featured large areas of solid colour, achieved a subtle brilliance, quite unlike the **Bizarre** range with its more direct impact.

The **Inspiration** range was created with a mixture of metallic oxide glazes to produce striking results in deep blues, turquoises, pinks and pale mauves. As the thin glaze tended to run, the pottery often became glued to the kiln furniture, causing time-consuming problems for the trimmers. Consequently, it was expensive and made in limited quantities.

Similarly, the **Applique** range was costly, as the designs painted in sumptuous colours (probably especially bought in), covered almost the entire surface of the ware. Vivid landscapes predominated, each with a castle, a windmill, a bridge or a stylised tree as the focal point, and it is this range which now fetches the highest prices at auction, being both rare and outstandingly attractive.

Much more widely used was the **Cafe Au Lait** technique, which being applied with a sponge gave a stippled surface to the pottery before a pattern was added on top or on an area left free from the stippling. Though its name suggests that only brown paint was used, yellow, green, orange and blue were also used very effectively.

Another successful technique was **Delecia**, which was originally comprised of random drippings of thin paint in a mixture of colours and was later combined with bands of fruit or flowers. Several factories used this method of covering the surface, but the stylish designs which came later are unique to Clarice Cliff. A popular landscape, **Forest Glen**, has **Delecia** as its background, while **Cherry Blossom** has a tree with white flowers against similar red and green runnings.

In **Nuage**, thickened paint was used to give a texture like orange peel, combined with bold, simple motifs that were produced with stencils, while **Damask Rose** aimed at the opposite effect, a perfectly smooth pink glaze with small decorations, which being difficult to apply, was produced only briefly. **Patina** went further than **Nuage**, as liquid clay or 'slip' was mixed with the paint to give a rough surface, on top of which the patterns, usually simple landscapes, were applied after glazing. Also uneven in surface, but no doubt much easier to decorate, was the **Scraphito** range, on which abstract designs were moulded deeply into the ware and then picked out in bold colours.

In the mid-Thirties, for the pattern **Rhodanthe** and its colour variations **Aurea** and **Viscaria**, and also for the thatched roof of **Trallee**, a method of blending brushstrokes of colour to create a shaded effect was used. Known as 'etching', this resulted in a softer, more subtle effect which was in keeping with popular taste. About this time the **Raffia** range was also launched. In this method the surface of the pottery was moulded to appear like woven raffia, a familiar handicraft material of the day, and colour was applied in patches in various combinations against glazes in pastel green and beige.

For **Goldstone**, a different type of body clay was used and a speckled surface achieved by mixing metallic dust into the glaze. Sometimes the decoration was restrained and the ware has the appearance of modern studio pottery, while other items have a rather garish form of decoration giving a dated look.

But perhaps the two ranges which most clearly indicate that the vivid colours of Clarice Cliff's early work had, for the time being, lost their appeal for contemporary purchasers are **My Garden** and **Celtic Harvest**. In January 1934, two years before the range began, Wilkinsons' took an advertisement in a publication for gardeners called 'My Garden', in which they described the **Goldstone** vases illustrated as being "designed by a lover of flowers for flower lovers", so quite possibly that was the origin of the name.

Popular both now and in their own day, **My Garden** with its pretty, un-sophisticated colours and moulded flowers, and **Celtic Harvest** with its encrusted fruit on handles and lids, were in production throughout the late Thirties and in the post-war years. Though they do not hold for collectors the strong appeal of early Bizarre shapes and patterns, they nevertheless illustrate the skill with which Clarice Cliff, as always, tailored her designs to satisfy prevailing taste, true to the adage of the day that 'the customer is always right' and reminding us that she was involved, first and foremost, in a com-mercial undertaking, in which she needed all her proven creative versatility to survive in a tough competitive market place.

Backstamps

So many and so varied are the backstamps to be found on Clarice Cliff pottery that they may well appear at first to be more of a hindrance than a help in deciding the date of any particular piece.

However, as long as collectors are not too dogmatic, backstamps can be a useful guide and a few general rules can be established.

Do not, for instance, be misled by impressed dates, since these refer to the date of manufacture of the pottery, not the date of its decoration. These two dates could be months or even a year or more apart. The hand-painted, stamped or litho-graphed information is what is relevant to the decoration.

Totally hand-painted marks can be found only on very early ware (i.e, the **Original Bizarre**) and only the earliest of these items do not credit Clarice Cliff. It was not long before her name was added, probably as an additional sales gimmick, to all wares. Colley Shorter must have been relieved that his talented protégé had a name which was easy to remember and with a good commercial ring. 'Handpainted Bizarre by Clarice Cliff, Newport Pottery, England' both sounded and read well in advertising and other promotional literature.

Once success was assured, a rubber stamp was used to speed up the marking process. At first this was quite a large size but later it was smaller and neater. These can be distinguished from later (1931) lithographs by the fuzzy outline of the rubber stamp and also, in some cases, by the colour of the ink used, since gilt and pale green occasionally appear as well as the usual black.

Even when lithographs, (which are pre-printed transfers), came into common use, pattern and range names were often added by hand, at first in script and later in block letters - unless the popularity of the pattern justified a lithograph of its own. Early **Crocus** and **Gayday** items have handwritten pattern names, while later pieces carry a lithograph of the name. Similarly, items with 'Registration applied for' obviously pre-date those with the eventual registration number added.

Bizarre Ware became increasingly popular, and from 1930 onwards some pottery was issued crediting Wilkinson's rather than the Newport Pottery. This was in order to spread tax liability. **Fantasque** as a range name was used between 1929 and 1934, at first on its own in two sizes, and later in combination with Bizarre, initially rubberstamped and later, from 1931 onwards, lithographed.

Biarritz, introduced in 1933, also had its own lithograph mark, and was used with a Newport or Wilkinson's backstamp according to where the piece was decorated, the Newport pieces having a Clarice Cliff or Bizarre mark added.

In the mid-Thirties, Clarice Cliff became involved in a time-consuming and far from successful experiment intended to involve leading artists of the day in the production of designs for tableware. Since a facsimile of the artist's signature was often included along with the other backstamps, these are an interesting reminder of a well-meaning but misguided attempt to bring fine art to the dining-table.

Among the artists involved were Dame Laura Knight, painter of fairground and circus subjects, Duncan Grant and Vanessa Bell of the Bloomsbury Group of artists and writers, Paul Nash who exhibited with the Surrealists, and Eva Crofts, the textile designer, as well as many others equally diverse. Gordon M Forsyth, from 1920 to 1945 Superintendent of Art Instruction in Stoke on Trent and an important influence on many pottery designers, also contributed to the experiment, the results of which eventually went on display in London in 1934 as 'Modern Art for the Table'. It later toured the country and it was taken to Australia.

Other interesting backstamps collectors may come across are those put on ware produced especially for stores like Harrods, Lawleys and Brice Rogers, whose orders were so large it was worthwhile adding their name on each item or, as in the case of Brice Rogers, a tiny picture of a quaint thatched cottage with the words, "Brice Rogers Cottage Pottery". The women's magazine, 'Woman's Journal', also commissioned patterns exclusive to their readers, and these dinner and tea sets occasionally appear in auction, identified by a backstamp giving the name of the magazine.

Finally however, after both the **Bizarre** and **Fantasque** marks had been phased out, various Clarice Cliff marks appeared alone, sometimes as lithographs and sometimes embossed on the ware itself. From 1941 the Newport mark was no longer used, as the factory had been requisitioned for the duration by the government, and once the sale of the factories to Midwinters was completed in 1964, all backstamps ceased. The plethora of backstamps tell a complicated story, and often add to the confusion, for it is possible to find a 23 piece tea-set of which only one item, perhaps the milk jug, carries any marks at all, while on another tiny item, like a coffee-cup, a wealth of backstamps may cover every scrap of space.

Nevertheless, together with a knowledge of pattern and shape chronology, backstamps can shed at least some light on the years when Clarice Cliff was at her busiest, little dreaming that 50 years later her work would be sought after by collectors worldwide.

Howard Watson

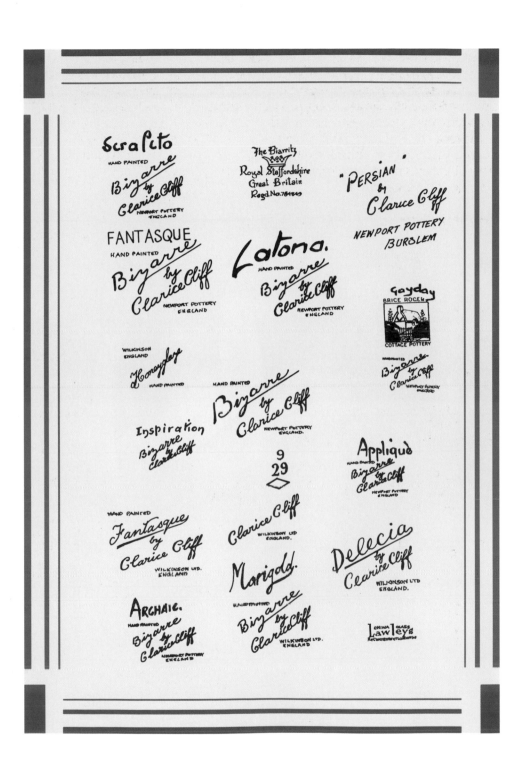

A Diamonds 370 vase (Courtesy of Christie's)

Original Bizarre vase, 370 (Courtesy of Christie's)

Inspiration vase, 370 (Courtesy of Christie's)

Inspiration coffee set, *Conical* (Collection of Des Jones)

Latona vase, 370 (Courtesy of Christie's)

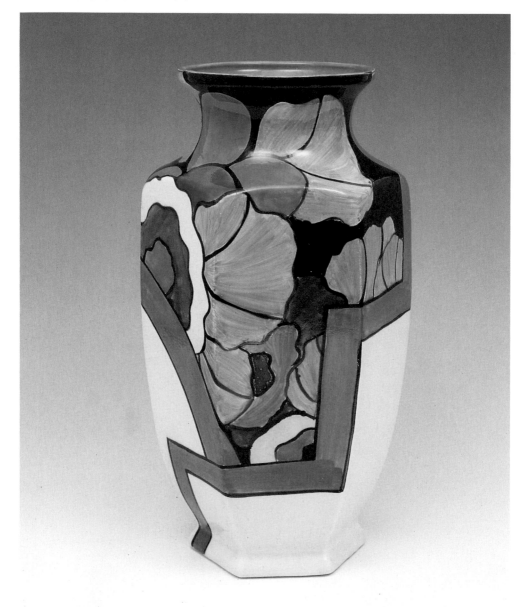

Latona Dahlia vase, 15 inches

Scraphito vase, 517 (Collection of Annie and Ian Tickler)

Applique Lugano Lotus jug (Collection of Annie and Ian Tickler)

Applique Avignon Lotus jug (Collection of Annie and Ian Tickler)

Delecia variations - **Original**, **Pansy** and **Citrus** (Courtesy of 'The Antique Dealer and Collectors Guide')

Forest Glen bowl 347 and vase 565

Delecia Anemone Isis vase

Nuage vases 205 and jampot (collection of Des Jones) with 10 inch plate

Damask Rose teapot, *Daffodil*

A **Blue Firs Patina** jardiniere with a **Blue Firs** table-centre. (Courtesy of Christie's)

Vase 341 in **Patina** Tree

Isis vase in **Patina** Country

Celtic Harvest items, a range increasingly popular

Bowl 367 in **Oranges Cafe Au Lait**

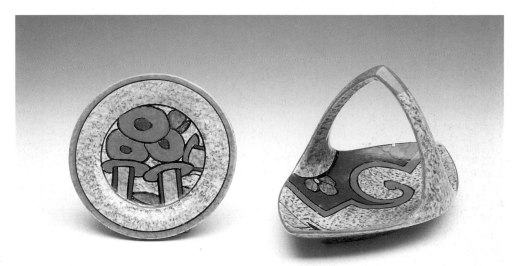

A biscuit plate in Bobbins **Cafe Au Lait** and a bon-bon dish, 471 with brown **Cafe Au Lait**

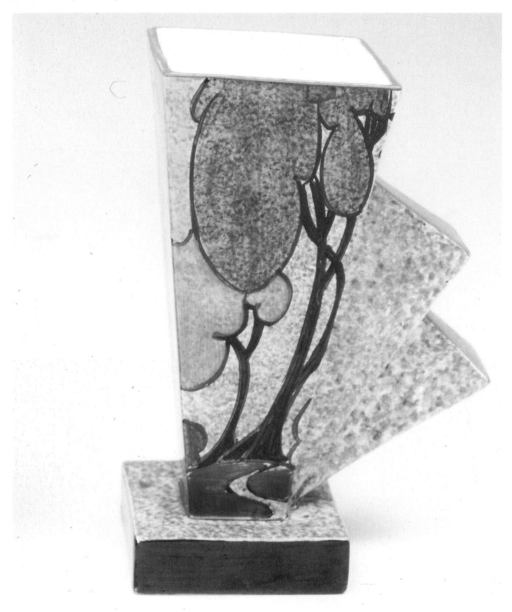

Autumn Cafe Au Lait on shape 461

Cowslip bowl, *Havre* shape, blue **Cafe Au Lait**

Nasturtium *Conical* sugar shaker and *Athens* jug

Rhodanthe Turkey Plate, 18 inches by 12 inches

An **Aurea** variation (no blue) on a tall *Bonjour* jug, and **Viscaria** on a *Daffodil* bowl

Goldstone Lynton coffee set (Courtesy of Johnathan Campbell)

Three early figurines, the two men each marked 'Clarice C 24' and the woman 'CC 24'
(Collection of Rosemary and David Temperley)

Two wallmasks, **Cleopatra** and a gypsy girl (Collection of Rosemary and David Temperley)

Three facemasks, the two smaller designed to be worn as pendants

Marlene, perhaps named after the film star Marlene Dietrich, and **Flora**

The **Age Of Jazz** figures, intended 'for use as a centre-piece when listening to a dance band on the wireless' (Courtesy of Muir Hewitt, Halifax Antiques Centre)

The **Lido Lady** ashtray 561, with a miniature version of **Blue Chintz** on the beach pyjamas

A rare **Showgirl** bookend. Her partner is said to have been a male dancer in top hat and tails

Applique Idyll wall-plaque, 13 inches. Made for Threlfalls Brewery and unusual in being signed on the front and in being the only Clarice Cliff figural pattern. (Courtesy of Sotheby's Chester)

Applique Idyll plaque for Threlfalls Brewery, signed on the front (Courtesy of Sotheby's, Chester)

Toby jugs, the largest being 10.5 inches (Items on right and foreground from the collection of Mike Harvey)

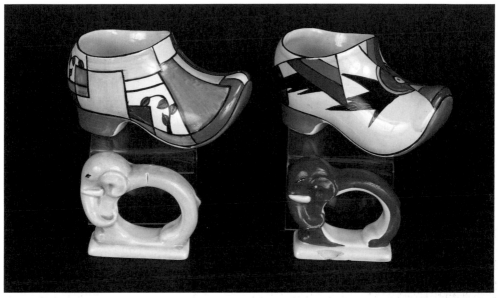

Sabots, or clogs, right in Lightning, left in Branch and Squares, with two elephant napkin rings (Courtesy of Christie's)

Moderne Cottage bookends 410 (Collection of Annie and Ian Tickler)

A Rooster teapot and two egg-cup sets. The duckling, in Lily Orange, would originally have had six egg cups.

A Chick cocoa pot with beaker and a Baby Ware teapot and plate, adapted from drawings by eight-year-old Joan Shorter. (Plate from Irene and Gordon Hopwood).

Signs of the Zodiac produced as wall decorations. (Aquarius and Sagittarius from the collection of Des Jones)

A sardine-box in **Original Crocus** shape 447

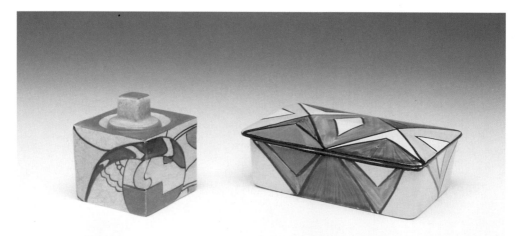

An inkwell and cigarette-box (Collection of Des Jones)

Conical sugar shakers - front row **Secrets**, **Hydrangea**, **Original Crocus**, **Blue Chintz** and **Banded**, back row, **Sungay**, **Bridgewater** and **Orange Autumn** (Courtesy of Christie's)

Advertising plaques for **Taormina**, **Aurea** And **Ferndale**, with a twin jamdish 531 in **Ferndale**

The larger of the two sizes of the White Swan flower-bowl

The larger of the two sizes of of the lilypad flower-bowl, usually pink or yellow but here in green

A plaque, 17 inches diameter, by Sir Frank Brangwyn R.A. representing life in Imperial India, presented to Brighton Museum in 1972 by Clarice Cliff (Courtesy of Royal Pavilion Art Gallery and Museums, Brighton)

A Dame Laura Knight 'totem pole' lampstand, featuring circus performers, presented to Brighton Museum in 1972 by Clarice Cliff. (Courtesy of Royal Pavillion Art Gallery and Museums, Brighton)

Dame Laura Knight - Six 'Circus' plates, probably an experimental colourway, usually pink, not blue. (Courtesy of Christie's)

A teapot and a tureen from the 'Circus' tableware designed by Dame Laura Knight (Collection of Rosemary and David Temperley)

A Dame Laura Knight cereal bowl, painted with a crowd of naked ladies

A bold design by Paul Nash (Courtesy of Christie's)

A **Biarritz** plate by Gordon Forsyth and a saucer by Eva Crofts

Varieties of **Crocus** teaware including an **Original Crocus** *Stamford* teapot, a **Purple Crocus** *Conical* teapot and a **Blue Crocus** *Bonjour* teapot with **Spring Crocus** teaplate, a Bunch **Crocus** Cup, Saucer and Teaplate, with **Peter Pan Crocus** items in the foreground. The **Lupin** vase is the only known example. The *Conical* salt and pepper shakers are **Sungleam**. (Courtesy of 'The Antique Dealer and Collectors Guide')

Two *Bonjour* teapots, **Banded** and **Coral Firs**, and a *Conical* teapot in **Oranges** (Courtesy of Christie's)

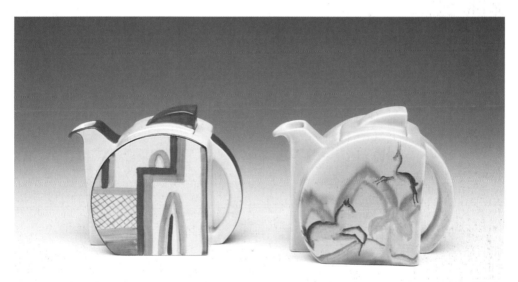

Two *Stamford* teapots, Tennis (from a private collection) and Stencilled Deer (Collection of Des Jones)

Dinnerware in **Lodore**, *Odilon* shape (Collection of Des Jones)

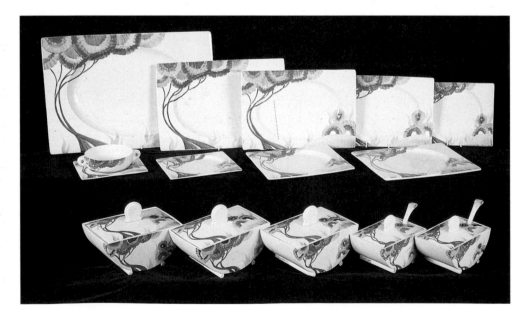

Dinnerware in **Rhodanthe, Biarritz** shape (Courtesy of Michael Newman)

Teapot, milk jug and sugar basin in **Kelverne**, *Trieste* shape (Courtesy of Ward Lock)

Conical **Ravel** breakfast ware

Tankard part coffee set in **Broth**

Early Morning set in **Sunray**, *Conical* shape with an unusual pierced handle, and other **Sunray** items (Courtesy of Christie's)

Lotus jug in Carpet (Collection of Jane Cook and Gary Withey)

Isis vase in **May Avenue** (Courtesy of Phillips)

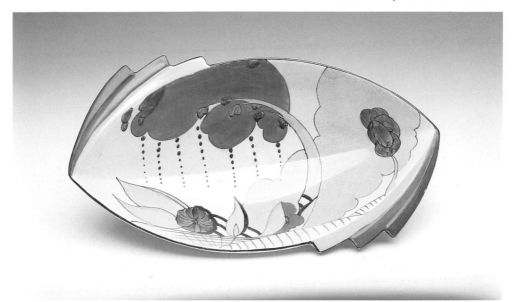

Devon bowl 475

Bridgewater bowl 475 (Collection of Diana York)

Marigold vase 386, 35.5cm (Collection of Des Jones)

Sliced Fruit stick stand, 27 inches (Courtesy of Phillips)

Woodland bowl, *Octagonal* shape

Blue Japan bowl, *Octagonal* shape (Collection of Diana York)

Tulip and Leaves Lotus jug (Courtesy of Christie's)

Rhodanthe Isis vase and two vases 183, and a Mei Ping 14 vase, a 120 vase and a 515 jardiniere in **House And Bridge** (Courtesy of Michael Newman)

A pair of 391 candleholders and a 610 candleholder in **Honolulu** (Courtesy of the 'Antique Dealer and Collectors Guide')

Bucket with inset drainer and matching *Tolphin* jug in **Orange Trees And House** (Collection of Annie and Ian Tickler)

A 460 vase in **Blue Chintz** (Collection of Diana York)

Arcahaic vase 375, **Summerhouse** 358 vase, Tennis *Athens* jug, **Berries** 363 vase, a 365 vase in **Latona** Tree and a 370 vase, in **Hollyrose** (Courtesy of Michael Yewman)

Mei Ping vase 14 in **Farmhouse** (Courtesy of Michael Newman)

Conical **Berries** jug (Collection of Annie and Ian Tickler)

Three Stamford teapots with milk jugs and sugar bowls in **House and Bridge**, **Red Autumn** and Orange Flower (Courtesy of Christie's)

Bonjour **Forest Leaves** breakfast set (Collection of Des Jones)

Summerhouse Isis vase, tapering vase in **Secrets**, Lotus jug and jardiniere in **Orange Autumn,** plate in **Orange House**, 120 vase in **Sunburst** and a Lotus jug in Diamonds (Courtesy of Phillips)

Large **Fragrance** plate, **Floreat** *Holborn* bowl, **Flora** *Stamford* tureen, **Coral Firs** Biarritz plate, bowl 383 in foreground, **House And Bridge** Octagonal plate with square bowl in **Newport** behind and *Conical* jug in Bobbins in front. Windbells bowl centre. (Courtesy of Phillips)

Blue Japan, Trallee and **Orange House** plates, **Summerhouse** 195 vase, **Mountain** large plate, **Trees And House** Lotus jug, **Farmhouse** vase 265 Beehive in **Yellow Autumn, Forest Glen** *Athens* jug, vase 362 in **Secrets**, shape 370 in **Farmhouse** and **Forest Glen** in shape 687 (Courtesy of Christie's)

Orange Roof Cottage wall plaque, 16.5 inches diam. (Courtesy of Phillips)

82

Wall plaque 13 inches diam. in Tulip and Leaves

Red Roofs on shapes 361 and 342

A *Dover* jardiniere and an *Octagonal* bowl in **Summerhouse**

A rare **Persian 1** bowl. **Persian 2** was in the **Inspiration** glaze

Perth jug in **Applique** Windmill

Moselle vase, shape 355

Cherry Blossom vase 572 and two **Honiton** items, the pattern produced by twirling a finger in the wet paint

A **Biarritz** plate with a floral design in red and black

A **Kandina** vase 355 (Collection of Des Jones)

Oranges And Lemons on an octagonal plate (Collection of Des Jones)

Octagonal bowl in Sliced Fruit

Lotus jugs with a **Canterbury Bells** jardiniere shape 515, two **Berries Cafe Au Lait** 187 vases and a **Melon** 370 vase (Courtesy of Michael Newman)

A large plate in **Green Chintz**, a flanged vase 465 in **Solitude** and a 450 *Daffodil* bowl in **Applique Idyll**, with other items (Courtesy of Phillips)

Autumn Lotus jug with green **Cafe Au Lait** (Collection of Annie and Ian Tickler)

A **Goldstone** vase & Yoo Hoo plate

A selection of vases (Courtesy of Christie's)

Key to Vases

Top row: Floral **Latona** shape 363, **Kandina** 358, **Inspiration** 362 **Pine Grove** 14, **Inspiration** 358, **Farmhouse** 362, **Inspiration** 355

Second row: **Pine Grove** 630, **Melon** 358, **Original Crocus** 358, **Honolulu** 451, **Melon** 358, **Blue Chintz** 268, **Latona** Prunus 369

Third row: **Orange Autumn** 465, **Melon** 205 **Floreat** 342, **Farmhouse** 451, **Aurea** 451 Garland 360, **Delecia Poppy** 379

Fourth row: **Delecia Citrus** 469, **Latona** Stained Glass 369, **Gardenia** 196, **Applique Orange Lucerne** 187

Fifth row: **Orange Chintz** 370, Orange Battle Cauldron, Geometric 186, **Patina** Country 370, **Gardenia** 371, **Melon** 341, **Patina** Country 265.

A pair of rectangular wall-plaques, an angel-fish lamp-base and two Lotus jugs (Courtesy of Sotheby's, Sussex)

Vase, embossed number 6028/s in **Passion Fruit**

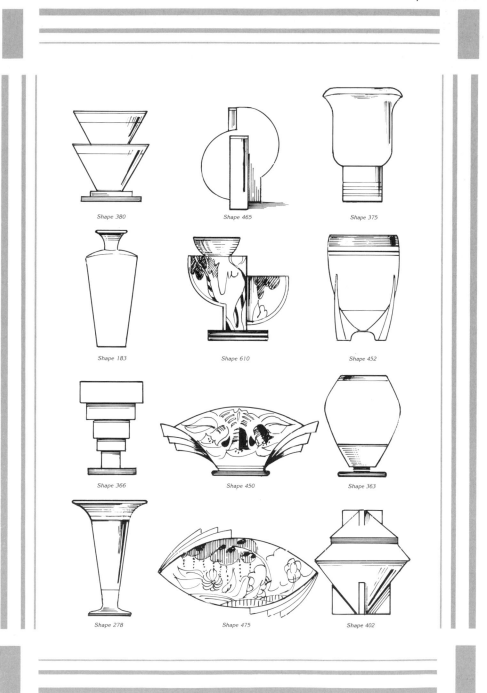

Shape 380

Shape 465

Shape 375

Shape 183

Shape 610

Shape 452

Shape 366

Shape 450

Shape 363

Shape 278

Shape 475

Shape 402

Conical

Bonjour

Stamford

Trieste

Lynton

Athens

Snail

Tankard

Conical

Bonjour

Daffodil

Lynton

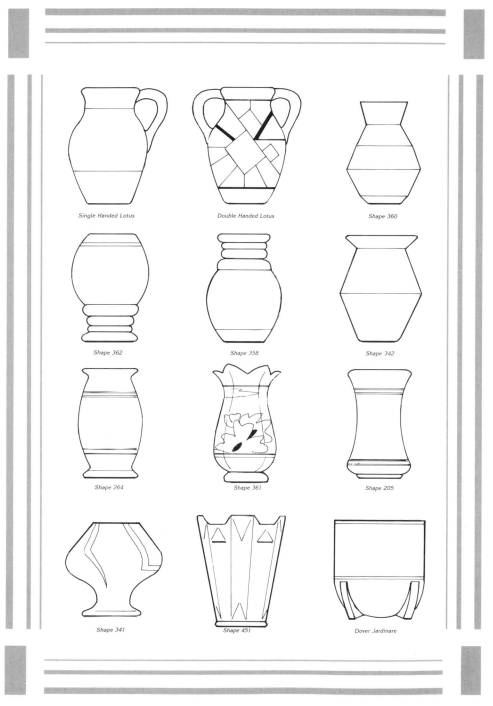

Single Handed Lotus

Double Handed Lotus

Shape 360

Shape 362

Shape 358

Shape 342

Shape 264

Shape 361

Shape 205

Shape 341

Shape 451

Dover Jardinare

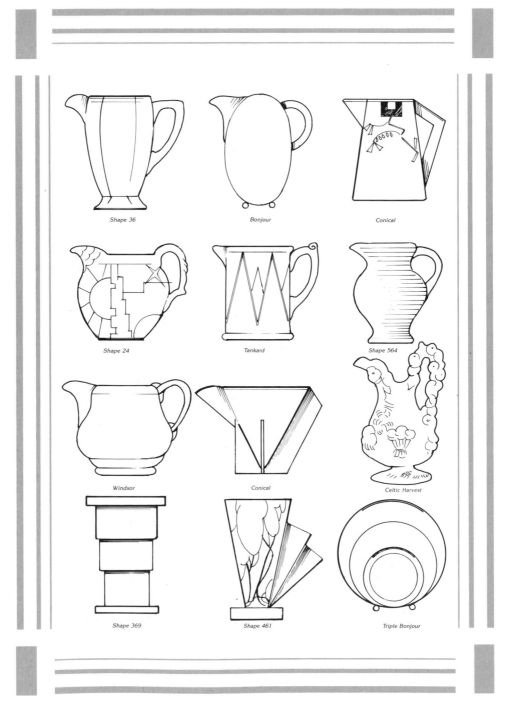

Shape 36   Bonjour   Conical

Shape 24   Tankard   Shape 564

Windsor   Conical   Celtic Harvest

Shape 369   Shape 461   Triple Bonjour

Shape 269

Shape 196

Isis

Shape 370

Mei Ping Vase Shape 14

Shape 441

Handled Jug

Bowl 515

Conical

Shape 379

Stamford Vase

Shape 464

Price and Pattern Guide

In preparing or using a price guide for Clarice Cliff pottery, it must be borne in mind that prices are bound to vary in accordance with collecting trends, with the economic climate, with regional disparities, and with different overheads and profit margins. However, what might be called the 'desirability factor' – remains surprisingly constant, so that if one item is worth today twice as much as another item, the proportion of their prices is likely to remain constant. Pattern, shape, and condition are the three factors which must be taken into consideration, with perfect pieces assumed in this guide.

Price Range 1 covers patterns fairly readily obtainable because they were made in considerable quantity. These include **Crocus, Gayday, Ravel, Rhodanthe** and similar. **Price range 2** covers patterns harder to find because they were made over a shorter length of time; either because of their complexity or through lack of popularity. These include **Melon, Gardenia, Gibraltar, Autumn** and similar. **Price range 3** covers rare patterns, including experimental wares, among them Appllique, **Tennis, Inspiration, Sunray, Solitude, Mountain** and similar. These are impossible to evaluate, since each must be taken on an individual basis, but a general attempt is made here on the basis of known sales.

Item	Price Range 1 (£)	Price Range 2 (£)	Price Range 3(£)
Teacup/saucer, open handle	55-95	100-150	150-250
Teacup/saucer, solid handle	75-130	125-175	200-300
Trio (cup/saucer/plate) open handle	100-150	135-195	200-350
Trio, solid handle	150-200	200-300	300-450
Coffee cup/saucer open handle	75-100	100-150	200-350
Coffee cup/saucer, solid handle	100-150	150-200	250-450
Plate, 9" size (Bread & Butter)	125-225	200-300	300-450
Teapots, Athens, Windsor, Lynton	200-300	250-350	350-500
Teapots, Bonjour, Conical, Stamford	350-450	400-550	600-800+
Teapots, Bonjour, Conical, Stamford with matching milk jug and sugar basin	450-600	550-700	700-1000
Bonjour, Conical, Stamford Early Morning Set (or Tea for Two), Teapot, milk jug, sugar basin, two cups/saucers and biscuit plate	700-800	750-900	850-1200+
Coffee-pot Tankard	200-300	300-400	500-750
Coffee-pot, Bonjour, Conical	300-400	350-500	500-800
Coffee Set: Coffee-pot, 6 cups/saucers milk jug, sugar basin, Bonjour, Conical (open handle slightly less)	600-850	850-1200	1500-3000
Jug, Athens, Conical	200-300	250-350	600-950+
Jug, Windsor, large	150-250	300-450	400-800
Jug, Bonjour, large	200-300	350-450	550-1000
Sugar Basin *Conical*, large	200-300	350-500	500-1000
Jampot, cylindrical, Bonjour	150-250	250-350	350-650

Beehive Honeypot, Apple Jampot, large	125-225	200-300	350-500
Beehive Honeypot, Apple Jampot, small	85-150	125-225	300-450
Sugar shaker, Conical, Bonjour	200-300	300-350	400-650
Plaque	300-400	400-550	700-1200
Cruet 3 items, Conical, Bonjour	150-250	300-400	400-600
Toastrack	100-200	200-300	300-450
Individual fruit dish, grapefruit dish	85-125	125-175	200-350
Biscuit Barrel	150-250	250-450	500-650
Wall-plate	200-300	300-600	600-1000+
Charger	350-500	500-750	800-2000+
Lotus Jug, large	400-650	650-1000	1500-3000+
Isis vase, large	400-650	650-1000	1500-3000+
Vase, e.g. shape 358, 361, 362etc	300-500	550-850	850-1000
Vase, rare shape with fins, flanges etc.	550-750	800-1000	1500-3000
Jardinere. planter	350-550	550-850	850-1200+
Bowl, large	150-300	300-400	600-800
Posy holder, long, circular	75-125	100-200	250-350
Coaster, ashtray	75-125	150-250	250-350
Candlestick, tall or ziggurat	150-250	300-400	400-600
Candleholder, small	100-150	150-250	250-350
Candleholder, Conical	150-200	200-300	300-500

Note: Smaller sizes of jugs, vases, bowls etc. pro rata.

FANCIES
Cigarette cups, card holders, clogs, serviettte rings, table centres, wallpockets, centre-pieces to hold flowers in a bowl, bookends, pencil holders etc. are also priced according to rarity, and, where applicable, pattern, e.g. Lilypad £225-300

LATER PATTERNS
Celtic Harvest, **My Garden**, mushroom glaze Items etc., though increasing in popularity, are still less expensive than other patterns, e.g. **Celtic Harvest** teapot £200-300, large jug, £150-225, small jug, £125-175.

NOVELTY TEAPOTS
Chick £200; Rooster £500-600; Wigwam £550-650

FACE MASKS
Price depends on subject, size and rarity, e.g. Chahar £1000-£2000+

AGE OF JAZZ FIGURES
Fetch very high prices because of their extreme rarity, say £2000-3000

Clarice Cliff Chronology

1899 Clarice Cliff born January 20, at 19 Meir Street, Tunstall, Staffordshire. The family later moved to Edwards Street, Tunstall.

Father:- Harry Thomas Cliff, an iron moulder. Mother:- Ann Cliff, née Machin. Brothers:- Harry, Frank. Sisters:- Sarah, Hannah, Dorothy, Ethel, Nellie.

1909 Left the High Street Elementary School to go to the Summerbank Road School.

1912 Left school to learn freehand painting at Lingard, Webster & Co., Swan Pottery, Tunstall.

1915 Left the Swan Pottery to learn lithography at Hollinshead & Kirkham, Unicorn Pottery, Tunstall. Attended evening classes at Tunstall School of Art, later transferring to Burslem School of Art.

1916 Joined A.J.Wilkinson's Royal Staffordshire Pottery, Burslem.

1920 Wilkinson's took over the Newport Pottery in Newport Lane, Burslem, adjoining their site. Clarice Cliff promoted to work as a gilder, with John Butler and Fred Ridgeway, Wilkinson's leading designers, on the Tibetan, Oriflamme and Rubaiyat ranges.

1923 The Wilkinson Archives has a note 'C.C. does the gold', referring to Pattern No.7309 on a plaque by Fred Ridgeway.

1924 Early figurines, including two men in Arab dress marked 'Clarice C 24' and an old market woman marked 'C.C.24'.

1925 Clarice Cliff moved to 40 Snow Hill, Hanley, a one-bedroom flat over a beauty salon. She was given a studio in Newport Pottery with facilities to produce the firm's publicity photographs. Comment was caused by her close association with Colley Shorter, the firm's managing director, a married man 17 years her senior.

1927 Between March 14 and May 26, Clarice Cliff took a short course in sculpture at the Royal College of Art at her employers' expense, her address being given as Campbell House, 90 Sutherland Terrace, Maida Vale, W8. Later this year she visited Paris, again at her employers' expense, to study Continental design. Returning to Newport Pottery, she began decorating a large stock of old-fashioned whiteware with brightly-coloured geometric patterns. A 15-year-old apprentice, Gladys Scarlett, assisted her.

1928 More apprentices - Annie Berrisford, Mary Brown, Nellie Harrison, Clara Thomas, Nancy Liversedge, Vera Rawlinson and Cissie Rhodes - joined the team, enabling a production line to be set up. Joan Shorter Baby Ware was launched, based by Clarice Cliff on drawings by Colley Shorter's eight-year-old daughter.

'Bizarre', the name chosen by Clarice Cliff, began to be used in July. Soon her name was added. The first press advertisement for **Bizarre Ware** appeared in August backed up by an in-store demonstration in London and a preview at the British Industries Fair.

In September, Ewart Oakes, Wilkinson's chief salesman, took **Bizarre Ware** to sell in Berkshire. His success led to more orders, and more apprentices, boys as well as girls, were added to the team.

A Bizarre backstamp was created, including Clarice Cliff's signature. Later this year **Crocus** began and continued in various versions until 1963. **Lupin** was also entered into the pattern-book but does not seem to have been put into production.

1929 **Fantasque** introduced as an additional range name.

Shapes: *Archaic* and *Conical*. Patterns

included Diamonds, Garland, Lightning, **Lodore, Kandina, Broth** (until 31) **Inspiration** (31) **Latona** (31) **Latona** Tree (30) **Lily** (30) **Ravel** (35) **Sunray** (30) **Trees And House** (31) **Umbrellas And Rain** (30) By the end of the year, the whole of the Newport Pottery was given over to **Bizarre Ware.**

1930 Shapes: *Stamford* and *Eton* tableware, **Age Of Jazz** figures. Patterns included Branch & Squares, Carpet, **Flora, Floreat,** Orange Battle, **Orange House, Persian (2),** Sliced Fruit, Sunburst, Tulip and Leaves, Yoo Hoo, **Applique Avignon** (until 31) **Applique Lucerne** (32) **Applique** Windmill (31) **Autumn** (34) **Berries** (31) **Inspiration Kinght Errant** (31) Latona **Dahlia** (31) **Melon** (33) **Oranges** (31) **Original Delecia (31) Scraphito (31).**

1931 Shapes: *Stamford* fancies and *Daffodil.* Conical sugar dredger **Nuage** and **Cafe Au Lait** techniques Patterns included: **Tennis, Marigold, Woodland, Applique Idyll** (until 35) Bobbins (33) **Farmhouse** (32) **Gardenia** (32) **Gibraltar** (32) **House & Bridge** (33) **Mountain** (32).

1932 Shapes: *Chick* cocoa pot and *Elephant* napkin rings **Patina** and **Damask Rose** techniques Patterns included **Forest Leaves, Holly Rose, Canterbury Bells** (until 33) **Chintz** (33) **Delecia Citrus** (33) **May Avenue** (33) **Orange Roof Cottage** (33) **Sungay** (33) Initiation of experiment to involve artists in production of designs for tableware.

1933 commissioned work from artists in production.
Shapes: *Bonjour* and *Biarritz* tableware.
Goldstone range, *Lynton* shapes, Blackbird pie funnels, facemasks **Marlene, Flora, Chahar** Patterns included Car And Skyscraper, **Devon, Japan, Solitude, Coral Firs** (until 36) **Cowslip** (34), **Delecia Pansy** (34) **Delecia Poppy** (34) **Honolulu** (34) **Secrets** (37) **Windbells** (34).

1934 Display of commissioned work -

'Modern Art for the table'. **Fantasque** phased out.
Shape: *Trieste*
Patterns included **Bridgewater, Newport,** Stencilled Deer, **Hydrangea** (until 35) **Moselle** (or 35) **Rhodanthe** (until 41 and post-war, **Viscaria** (36).

1935 Late in the year, Bizarre phased out. Patterns included **Fragrance, Pine Grove, Aurea** (until 37) **Cherry Blossom** (36) **Trallee** (36).

1936 Patterns included **Kelverne, Passion Fruit, Forest Glen** (until 37) **Honiton** (37) **My Garden** (until 41 and Post-war) **Raffia** (37) **Taormina** (37).

1937 Shapes: *Windsor,* Gnome Nursery Ware.
Patterns included **Ferndale, Delecia Anemone** (38).

1938 Shapes: **Celtic Harvest** (until 41 And Post-war), Waterlily Range, Signs Of The Zodiac.

1939 September, outbreak of war.
November 2 death of Mrs Annie Shorter.

1940 December 21, Marriage Of Clarice Cliff And Arthur Colley Austin Shorter (not Announced Until November 1941).

1941 Newport Pottery requisitioned by the government.

1942 No more decorated pottery for the duration of the war.

1945 Ending of hostilities. Decorated pottery resumed for export only. Restrictions gradually eased.

1952 Wartime restrictions finally lifted completely. Coronation ware produced.

1963 December - Colley Shorter died, aged 81.

1964 Factories sold to Midwinters and Clarice Cliff retired.

1972 Brighton Museum held the first British exhibition of Clarice Cliff pottery, to which she contributed catalogue notes and items from her own collection, some of which she later gave to the Museum.
October 23, Clarice Cliff died after a brief illness, aged 73.

Appendix - A Note on Specialist Auctions

It is interesting to compare the highspots, in terms of prices paid (including premium) at each of three Christie's sales over a period of some 20 months. The cover of the catalogue for the sale in March, 1989, carried a photograph of items in the **Sunray** pattern, and these certainly attracted very good bids - a jardiniere over £3500, a tea for two nearly £3000 and a pair of vases almost £4000 - but other patterns also held their own. An **Inspiration** coffee service with gilt interiors fetched over £5000, and six Laura Knight Circus plates in an unusual colourway reached £11000, as against an estimate of £1000-1500. Another surprise was a **May Avenue** vase, estimated to fetch £600-1000, which in the event realised over £6000.

In November the same year the catalogue cover carried **Applique** items in dazzling array - there had been no **Applique** in the previous sale. Once again these realised excellent prices, an **Applique Lugano** *Conical* jug bringing close to £4000 in spite of a hairline crack to the rim, and a nine-inch plate in **Applique Windmill** reaching more than £4000. But here again there were surprises. **May Avenue** remained popular at nearly £2500 for a *Daffodil* jug and commissioned work was still attracting high bids - £8500 for a set of beer pitcher and six tankards by Dame Laura Knight and over £7000 for a matching 18 inch circular dish.

In the October sale of the following year a mixture of highly desirable items were shown on the front cover of the catalogue, including **Sunray**, **Applique** and **Luxor**, with an array of *Conical* shakers, ranging from **Crocus** to **May Avenue** on the back cover. (Kept until last, the **May Avenue** shaker fetched almost £2000.) This time, however, no doubt owing to the prevailing economic climate, prices did not rise so high, though an **Applique Caravan** plate brought over £2000 and a Laura Knight Circus teapot £2500.

A word of caution on auctions is necessary, however, as the auction room atmosphere may well bring out hidden rivalries, leading to artificially high prices as two or more bidders get locked into a battle for one item. The resulting tension encourages higher and higher bids, and the final purchase price may well be far more than the piece could have realised in calmer circumstances. Also the catalogue illustrations inevitably tend to focus on certain lots to the disadvantage of others, since not every lot can be illustrated. An eye-catching cover can be made by selecting a group of spectacular items which then become the most talked about and sought after pieces in the sale.

Now that the economy is recovering, it will be interesting to see what are the highspots of the forthcoming Christie's sales. No doubt, some items will attract maximum attention, but there are always some reasonable buys and even the occasional bargain for the collector able to keep his head and make appropriate bids.

Bibliography

'Clarice Cliff' (exhibition catalogue) Brighton Museum and Art Gallery, 1972 - occasionally available from antiquarian booksellers

'Clarice Cliff' Peter Wentworth Sheilds & Kay Johnson, L'Odeon, London 1976 & 1981

'Bizarre - Pottery by Clarice Cliff' (auction sale catalogue) second edition, priced, Christie, Manson & Woods, Ltd., London 1983

'Clarice Cliff, the Bizarre Affair' Louis Meisel & Leonard R. Griffin, Thames & Hudson, 1988

'Collecting Clarice Cliff' by Howard Watson, Kevin Francis Publishing, 1988

'Clarice Cliff', auction sale catalogue 20/03/89 Christie's, South Kensington

'Clarice Cliff', auction sale catalogue 6/11/89 Christie's, South Kensington

'Clarice Cliff', auction sale catalogue 22/10/90 Christie's, South Kensington

All quarterly reviews and publications by The Clarice Cliff Collectors Club, editor, Leonard R. Griffin.

'British Pottery, An Illustrated Guide' Geoffrey A. Godden, Barrie & Jenkins, 1974

'A Collector's History of English Pottery', Griselda Lewis, Antique Collectors Club (third edition) 1985

'Art Deco Tableware' Judy Spours, Ward Lock, 1988

Patterns Index

Applique Avignon	25	
Applique Idyll	44, 45, 91	
Applique Lugano	24	
Applique Orange Lucerne	94	
Applique 'Windmill'	85	
Archaic	76	
Aurea	36, 51, 94	
Autumn Cafe Au Lait	34, 92	
Banded	51, 59	
Berries	76, 78	
Berries Cafe Au Lait	90	
Blue Chintz	42, 51, 75, 94	
Blue Crocus	58	
Blue Firs	29	
Blue Japan	71, 81	
'Bobbins'	80	
'Bobbins' Cafe Au Lait	33	
'Branch & Squares'	47	
Bridgewater	51, 67	
Broth	63	
'Bunch' Crocus	58	
Canterbury Bells	90	
'Carpet'	65	
Celtic Harvest	32	
Cherry Blossom	87	
Coral Firs	4, 59, 80	
Cowslip	35	
Damask Rose	29	
Delecia Anemone	27	
Delecia Citrus	26, 94	
Delecia Pansy	26	
Delecia Poppy	94	
Devon	67	
'Diamonds'	18, 80	
Farmhouse	77, 81, 94	
Ferndale	51	
Flora	80	
Floreat	80, 94	
Forest Glen	26, 81	
Forest Leaves	79	
Fragrance	80	

Gardenia	94	
'Garland'	94	
Geometric	94	
Gibraltar	4	
Goldstone	37, 93	
Green Chintz	91	
Hollyrose	76	
Honiton	87	
Honolulu	74, 94	
House & Bridge	73, 79, 80	
Hydrangea	51	
Inspiration	20 94	
Inspiration Knight Errant	4	
Kandina	88, 95	
Kelverne	61	
Latona	21	
Latona Dahlia	22	
Latona 'Floral'	94	
Latona 'Prunus'	94	
Latona 'Stained Glass'	94	
Latona 'Tree'	76	
'Lightning'	47	
Lily Orange	48	
Lodore	60	
Lupin	53	
Marigold	68	
May Avenue	66	
Melon	90, 94	
Moselle	86	
Mountain	81	
Nasturium	35	
Newport	80	
Nuage	28	
Orange Autumn	51, 80, 94	
'Orange Battle'	94	
Orange Chintz	94	
'Orange Flower'	79	
Orange House	80, 81	
Orange Trees & House	74	
Orange Roof Cottage	82	
Oranges	59	

Oranges & Lemons	89	
Oranges Cafe Au Lait	33, 59	
Original Bizarre	19	
Original Crocus	50, 51, 58, 94	
Original Delecia	26	
Passion Fruit	96	
Patina Blue Firs	29	
Patina 'Country'	31, 94	
Patina 'Tree'	30	
Persian 1	85	
Persian 2	4	
Peter Pan Crocus	58	
Pine Grove	94	
Purple Crocus	58	
Ravel	62	
Red Autumn	79	
Red Roofs	84	
Rhodanthe	36, 60, 73	
Scraphito	23	
Secrets	51, 80, 81	
'Sliced Fruit'	69, 89	
Solitude	91	
Spring Crocus	58	
'Stencil Deer'	59	
Summerhouse	76, 80, 81, 84	
'Sunburst'	80	
Sungay	51	
Sungleam	58	
Sunray	64	
Taomina	51	
'Tennis'	59, 76	
Trallee	81	
Trees & House	81	
'Tulip & Leaves'	72 83	
Viscaria	36	
Windbells	80	
Woodland	70	
Yellow Autumn	81	
'Yoo Hoo'	93	

' ' Denotes unofficial pattern names, now popularly accepted.

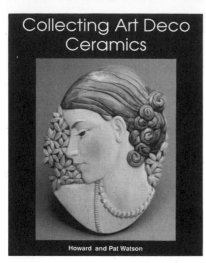

Collecting Art Deco Ceramics.
Due out in 1992
Hardback and paperback
by Pat Watson

The Beswick Price Guide
Due out in 1992
Hardback and paperback
by Harvey May

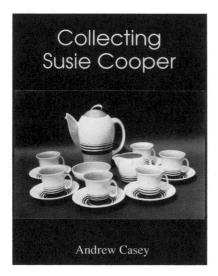

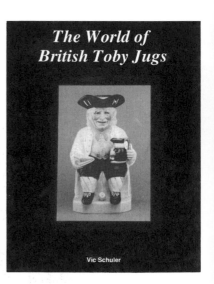

Collecting Susie Cooper
Due out in 1992
Hardback and paperback
by Andrew Casey

Collecting British Toby Jugs
Due out in 1992
Hardback and paperback
by Vic Schuler

Kevin Francis have been producing books on British ceramics for many years.
The books shown above are just a few of the titles due to come out in 1992.
Others include *The Character Jug Collectors Handbook 5th edition*,
The Doulton Figure Collectors Handbook 3rd edition and
The David Winter Cottages Handbook 1st edition.

For details of publication dates & prices write to Kevin Francis, Landcroft House, 85 Landcroft Rd, London SE22 9JS

COLLECTOR'S BIZARRE

CLARICE CLIFF SPECIALISTS

SELL US YOUR UNWANTED ITEMS

ONE PIECE OR A COMPLETE COLLECTION

WE BUY WITH DISCRETION

FOR HELP OR ADVICE
PLEASE RING JULIAN OR TRACEY ON
0527 - 70627 24 HOUR LINE
0831 - 800 - 488 MOBILE PHONE

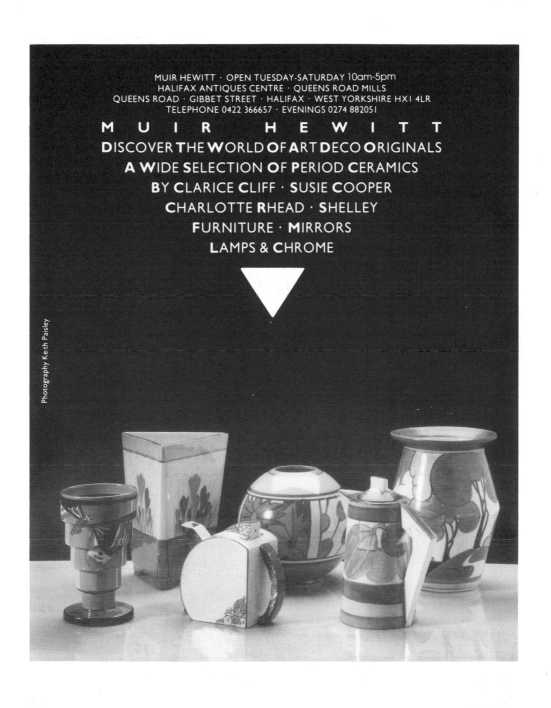